PLAYLAND

in Photos

Ocean City Amusement Park Memories

SHORES

Playland on an early 1970s summer morning.

To all of our cherished Ocean City memories, and to all of the lost Ocean City landmarks where they took place...

Praise for PLAYLAND

Greetings From Ocean City, Maryland

"PLAYLAND takes you back to a time when Ernie's Donuts were always hot and delicious, the Admirals played at the Pier Ballroom, and a great amusement park existed on 65th Street. It's a great beach read!" - **Hunter "Bunk" Mann, author,** *Vanishing Ocean City* **and** *Ghosts in the Surf*

"Weaving two stories together, one from his childhood, the other as a young man working during the summer, Earl Shores brings Ocean City, Maryland to life, vividly, as it was during the 60s, 70s, and 80s." - **Sandy Hurley, curator, Ocean City Maryland Life-Saving Station Museum**

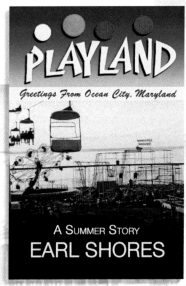

"There is a world-famous amusement park in Rye, NY, called *Playland*, but sure as the salty goodness of Thrasher's fries or a hole-in-one at Old Pro Golf, it's not the only Playland worth writing about. And just like those Ocean City Boardwalk icons, writer Earl Shores captures the exquisite nostalgia of Playland on 65th Street, one of OC's original family-fun amusements destination." - **Coastal Style Magazine**

"PLAYLAND far exceeds all expectations by transporting readers to a simpler time in Ocean City history, and our society in general. All OCMD local residents and tourists alike will get a kick out of reminiscing while enjoying this truly great body of work." - **Brandon Seidl, founder, Trimper's Haunted House Online, co-founder, The Bill Tracy Project, co-author,** *Trimper's Rides* **and** *Ocean City Oddities*

"Most of us have a defining summer of our youth. Earl Shores take us back to his special summer in 1980 when he lived in the seaside resort of Ocean City, Maryland and worked as a ride operator at Playland, a long gone amusement park. It turned out that this would be the final summer that Playland operated and Shores takes us back to the park with his vividly descriptive style of storytelling. The rides, the co-workers and the customers provide a rich tapestry of a long gone place that provided so many memories and shaped a person's life forever." - **Jim Futrell, historian, National Amusement Park Historical Association**

"PLAYLAND transports us back to a time when summers were magical and friendships were made and renewed year after year. The words put into motion an emotional ride that allows us to check-off a bucket list item that ceased to exist long ago. Read the book, close your eyes, and realize that 'Playland' still exists." - **Rick Machado, Playland alumnus 1976-80**

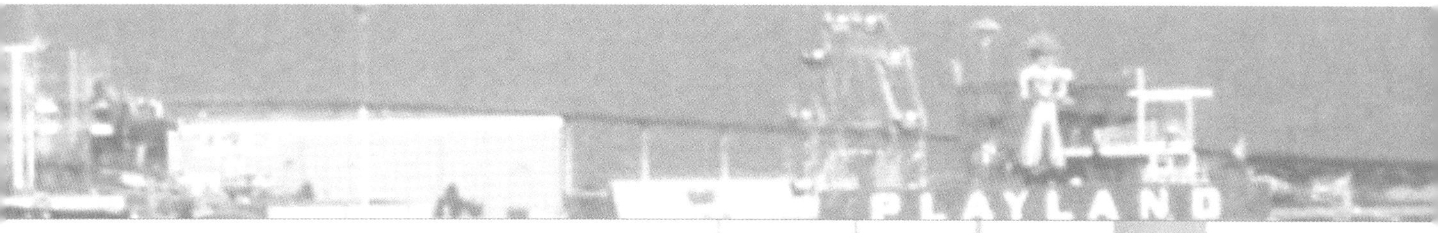

Contents

Earl Shores/One Way Road Press

P.O. Box 371

Media, PA 19063

www.onewayroadpress.com

Cover Design & Interior Design by Earl Shores

Playland In Photos: Ocean City Amusement Park Memories/ Earl Shores – 1st ed.

978-0-9892363-7-9

Introduction

The **Playland Amusement** Park was an Ocean City, Maryland landmark from 1965 to 1980. Located on a vast bayside lot at 65th Street, Playland evolved from being a lonely "up the beach" amusement oasis in 1965 to sitting almost dead center along a fully-developed seven-mile coastline by the time the park gates closed for good in 1980.

After toughing out some lean early years, Playland received a fortuitous boost from Maryland highway planners, who decided to run a second road crossing into Ocean City at 62nd Street. Once the centipede-like Route 90 bridge opened in 1971, Playland was the landmark that vacationers' eyes were drawn to as they traveled eastward into Ocean City – especially at night when the illuminated park rides lit up the sky, casting colorful reflections onto the shimmering canvas of the Assawoman Bay.

As I discovered after publishing *PLAYLAND: Greetings From Ocean City, Maryland*, in 2019, the park still holds special memories for a surprisingly large number of people. Even for those who made only a single visit to Playland, there was something about the self-contained location and unique collection of rides that turned a day in the park into a lifetime memory.

Playland had an extensive Kiddie Land throughout its fifteen years of life, and the only wooden coaster to ever exist in Ocean City. It also had the Monster Mouse, the ride with the highest and steepest drop in all of OC. And then there was the Ghost Ship, a two-story Bill Tracy-designed dark ride that has attained mythical status among amusement park aficionados.

Oh yes, and starting in 1978, Playland was home to "Ocean City's Largest Go-Kart Track." I knew this from the large red-lettered advertising signs that buzzing single-engine prop planes labored to pull up and down the beach every day. I also knew it from the Playland radio commercials that 100 KHI played at least once an hour.

But I came to know this fact intimately from the six-week stint I spent running those well-advertised go-karts in 1980, the "buzz" of my summer Playland position quickly dissipating in the nightly haze of exhaust fumes that groups of free-ranging riders spewed onto our floodlit track.

Fortunately, I was pardoned from my exile to Playland's tire-lined L-shaped asphalt in late July. From that point on, I ran over a half-dozen of the park's main attractions and had one of the best summers of my life. Even with the go-karts, working at Playland was the best job I ever had, in what I think was one of the most scenic locations ever to exist in Ocean City.

I'm not the only one who feels that way. Most of the Playland alumni I've interacted with through the years view working in the park as a once in a lifetime opportunity. And we all agree that we were lucky to have had such an experience.

From all the stories that were shared on my Playland Facebook page (facebook.com/Playland-BookOCMD), I started wondering whether a photo book was a feasible idea. I'd collected dozens of park images while writing PLAYLAND: *Greetings From Ocean City, Maryland.* But were they really of enough quality to create a captivating book?

The answer came when the National Amusement Park Historical Association published a Playland article I wrote for their *Chronicle* magazine. The six-page layout was beautiful, celebrating Playland in a printed full-color splendor that only existed previously in my memories.

And there was no question about it – a Playland photo book had to be done.

So while this book is a meticulous look at Playland using the currently available historical records, it is far from a complete history of the park. But I think the images bring Playland to life, making you want to step inside of each page.

Those of us who worked at Playland during its final summer had no idea the park would never re-open. Everything seemed normal right up to the end. Most of us punched out on our last day without a thought that this was the last time we'd ever see the park.

It's a loss that many of us have carried through the years. Something was there...and then suddenly wasn't, an unfortunate Ocean City routine that has played out many times during the last four decades. And there's no doubt that after watching so many touchstones from my Ocean City experience disappear, this book and *Greetings From Ocean City* are my personal attempts to take one final walk around Playland, determined to savor every step and every moment, even while chasing down wayward riders on the go-karts.

I hope you enjoy *Playland In Photos*. May you find your own special piece of Ocean City inside its pages.

PLAYLAND

AMUSEMENT PARK

65th Street, Ocean City, Maryland
1965

Ghost Ship

Broadway Trip

Airborne

Monorail

Antique Cars

Kiddie Whip

Pony Carts

Tubs-O-Fun

Kiddie Boats

Space Age

Motorcycles

Helicopters

Kiddie Coaster

Fire Trucks

Food Stand

Tank Ride

Hennecke Auto Carousel

Old 99 Train

Playland Pirate →

OCEAN PLAYLAND

Photo by F.W. Brueckmann - Published by

AT THE FUN PARKS

New Ocean City Park Set

The vast ride complex known as Ocean Playland (AB, April 17) has its debut scheduled for May 28 in Ocean City, Md. Extensive promotion tactics are being used, including radio, TV, newspapers, billboards, airplane banners, bumper stickers and search-lights. Treasurer Oscar Carey expressed optimism for a successful initial season, pegging attendance at a minimum of 700,000 persons. The park is said to fill a definite vacuum and will be the largest fun installation on the Del-Mar-Va peninsula.

Amusement Business, May 29, 1965

OCEAN PLAYLAND BUILDS—The new fun park at Ocean City, Md., was in midst of building-stage last week, but expects to open May 28 with about 50 to 53 days' work still ahead. At left, with Sky Rider terminal in background, progress is viewed by Pete Barnes of Universal Design, Ltd.; Carlos Freeman, construction engineer; Jim Gross, superintendent and park manager, and Oscar Carey, park treasurer. At right, crane hoists Douglas fir timber from Oregon. Cadmium bolts will join pieces. Oil-base paint was used first, then water-base paint. Seven key parkmen, 12 helpers are on job.

Early reporting done by the trade publication Amusement Business as Playland was being constructed in the spring of 1965. From the National Amusement Historical Association archives (above) and the Karl Schwarz Playland archive (below).

OCEAN PLAYLAND—Crane's-eye view shows part of new park, with 17 rides in picture. Clockwise from left are Lover's Coach, Hi-Rider loading area, Dark Ride, disassembled Broad-way Trip, Airborne, Monorail, Antique Cars, kiddieland, Ferris Wheel. Harassed realtor, left, is Jim Caine, of group promoting park. He hollers to truck arriving with equipment. (AB photos)

Beginnings

Ocean Playland was designed and laid out by Allen Hawes, the owner of Wildwood, New Jersey ride maker Universal Design Ltd. Hawes had been hired by local real estate developer and Playland majority owner Jim Caine, who also gave Hawes roles as advisor and purchasing agent.

With Hawes in charge of ride selection it's little surprise that the 860 ft. x 375 ft. westward pointing strip of man-made land that Playland occupied was encircled by a UDL Satellite Monorail ride. And that the new park also had a UDL Hi-Rider Sky Ride bisecting the back half of the property, and a UDL Bill Tracy-designed two-story dark ride, which ended up being the legendary Ghost Ship.

The park was physically impressive. As a goggle-eyed youngster I was overwhelmed while walking under the horizontal "Ocean Playland" sign, on top of which sat a towering bearded pirate, the figure being an iconic 20-foot tall "Muffler Man" from the International Fiberglass Co.

Once inside the gates and past the Ferris wheel (Garbrick's initially, upgraded to a larger Eli wheel in 1967), there was an elaborate Kiddie Land in the front right corner of the park, consisting of a Chance Old 99 Train, a beautiful and rare German-built Hennecke Auto Carousel, a Schiff's Kiddie Coaster, and a trio of Hampton umbrella rides (Space Age, Tubs-O-Fun, and Motorcycles). There were also Pony Carts, a Kiddie Whip, and Fire En-

Playland's iconic International Fiberglass Co. "Muffler Man" pirate guards the park in the fall of 1966. Playland had a seasonal schedule that ran from mid-May to Labor Day.

PLAYLAND

BALLOONS

CLOSED

A 1965 Ocean City Visitor advertisement. Visible from this Sky Ride perspective are the Trabant/ Satellite ride, the Ghost Ship and Broadway Trip (left), and the Old Pro Circus Golf Course.

Another 1965 Ocean City Visitor ad with a fantastic panorama of Kiddie Land. The Fire Engine ride is in the foreground. Next are the Helicopters, Kiddie Coaster, the trio of Hampton umbrella rides (Tubs-O-Fun, Space Age, and Motorcycles), and the upper covering of the Kiddie Boats.

gines from Mangels, Kiddie Boats and Helicopters from Herschell's, as well as an elaborate Antique Car set-up from Morgan Hughes.

And the rest of the park was completely mesmerizing as well. Right beside Kiddie Land was the Lover's Coach (Hughes), a swing-like ride that loaded on the ground and then lifted straight up into the air as the two-seater coaches revolved around the center support piece. Then just beyond the Antique Cars was the Airborne (Hughes), which at first glance, looked like a grounded Paratrooper ride before spinning and rising majestically into the air, moving with a gracefulness that no Paratrooper could match.

Past the Airborne on the right was the Broadway Trip, a box-shaped funhouse that I was only able to see from the outside in 1965. It did look like fun, having a two-story tall staircase as an entrance and a long metal slide as an exit. Joined to the Broadway Trip was the warehouse-sized Ghost Ship, its creepy building-length façade featuring a splintered, sail-less wooden galleon being devoured by a giant skeleton-faced crab.

Directly across from these two rides, occupying a rectangular space in the center of the park, was the Old Pro Circus Mini-Golf Course, complete with a bright yellow Circus Train "clubhouse." Sitting at the western edge of the course was a Chance Trabant, whose round shape led you to the back bayside corner of the park where the intimidating Herschel Monster Mouse dared riders to take on the biggest vertical drop in all of Ocean City. To the left of the Mouse, centered between a pair of Sky Ride towers, was the oval track of the gas-engine powered Hot Rods (Hughes).

Finally, in the southern corner of the park, rising up like a white serpent, was the Hurricane. As wooden coasters go it was on the small side, with a 40-foot drop and a tight figure-eight layout. Yet even with its compact size, it rumbled and whooshed like a larger coaster. And it would turn out to be the only wooden coaster ever to exist in Ocean City.

Out in the bay beyond the Hurricane was the Ocean Trip U-Drive Boats (Hughes), a ride where individual go-kart sized boats could be driven around in a large piling-enclosed pen. Rounding out the rides was a permanent cinder block pavilion that housed the sporty-looking Reverchon Dodge-em cars. Playland's other buildings were filled out with carnival games and food concessions.

A surprising thing to learn about these early years was that each ride was individually owned and "booked in" for the summer. It was a novel arrangement the trade magazine *Amusement Business* noted in an article about Playland in May of 1965, stating that industry observers were watching closely to see if Playland could "overcome the handicaps of an all-independent operation."

Despite this impressive lineup of rides and acres of free parking, Playland struggled with attendance during the early years of the park. This wasn't a total surprise, or at least it shouldn't have been, considering that the park was 35 blocks north of the just-opening Jolly Roger Amusement Park, and over 60 blocks north of Ocean City's main amusement area, which in 1965 consisted of the Pier and Trimper's Rides at the southern end of the boardwalk.

A 1965 bayside bird's eye view of Playland. The full scope and size of the park is on display, including the parallel midways that gave access to the rides. The north midway is on the left, the south midway on the right.

65th STREET PLAYLAND

OCEAN CITY, MARYLAND

In Maryland – it's Ocean City for Fun
Million Laughs . . . Thousand Thrills . . .

Bring Your Youngsters—Fun for All—Admission Free

FREE PARKING AT OCEAN PLAYLAND

In 1965, Playland sometimes ran multiple advertisements in a single issue of the Ocean City Visitor. This ad had a Sky Ride view of the Hurricane Coaster. Its figure-eight layout was built from National Amusement Device Company plans and blueprints. National Amusement Device also provided the cars for the ride. The drop of the first hill was reported at the time to be 40 feet.

OCEAN PLAYLAND AMUSEMENT PARK
65th. ST. OCEAN CITY, MD.

Courtesy of Brian Kerr

The unique Lover's Coach was made by the Morgan Hughes company. A rare ride, it was only in Playland during the inaugural 1965 season. At night it was spectacular to watch.

Morgan Hughes also made Playland's Airborne. A more common ride than the Lover's Coach, the Airborne was part of the park right up until Playland closed in 1980.

Looking down Playland's north midway toward the bay in October of 1966. Most of the rides have been taken apart and fully wrapped for the coming winter weather. In the center of the park (behind the ticket booth), a go-kart track has replaced the Lover's Coach.

All of these Playland ads and images appeared in the Beachcomber during the summer of 1966.

OCEAN PLAYLAND

65th St., On The Bay

OCEAN CITY'S ONLY ROLLER COASTER

Thrill To The MONORAIL TRAIN & SKYRIDE

Free Admission - Free Parking for 1000 Cars

OPEN   WEEKDAYS - SAT. & SUN.
at 5 PM   at Noon

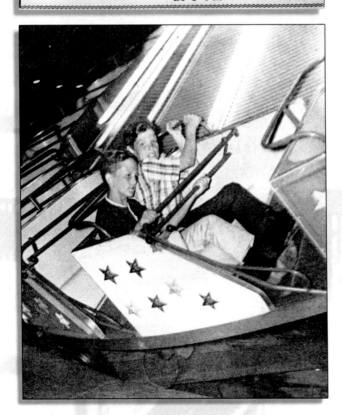

OCEAN PLAYLAND

IN OCEAN CITY
65th & OCEAN HIWAY

Roller Coaster—Monorail
Ferris Wheel—Monster Mouse
Hot Rod Car—Miniature Golf
Sky Ride—Antique Autos
Rides For Adults & Children
Games of Skill — Fun Houses

FREE ADMISSION

FREE PARKING FOR 1,000 CARS

A winterized Kiddie Land in October of 1966. The basin for the Kiddie Boats is empty (left), and the Kiddie Whip (center) has been taken down to its oval platform. The Broadway Trip building is also missing at this point, having been disassembled and sent to Pirate's World in Florida.

The Famed Monorail Ride

OCEAN PLAYLAND
65th St., On The Bay
OCEAN CITY'S ONLY ROLLER COASTER
Thrill to the MONORAIL TRAIN & SKYRIDE
Free Admission - Free Parking for 1000 Cars
OPEN   WEEKDAYS—SAT. & SUN
at 5PM   at Noon

65th STREET PLAYLAND
OCEAN CITY, MARYLAND

In Maryland – it's Ocean City for Fun
Million Laughs . . . Thousand Thrills . . .
Bring Your Youngsters—Fun for All—Admission Free

FREE PARKING AT OCEAN PLAYLAND

More Playland advertisements and images from the Beachcomber during the summer of 1966 (above and top right). The ad on the right is from a 1965 Visitor.

Ocean Playland's Key: Promotions

The Long View—Management's aim is to fill yawning midway with visitors.

Biggest problem for Ocean Playland in Ocean City, Md., has been drawing patrons northward from the downtown boardwalk complex. In the park's third season, a new management team (AB, June 17) has tackled the problem diligently.

Playland opened in 1965 with a concept of independently owned rides, but this has been modified sharply. Several have been acquired by the park corporation and policy control has become more effective as the independents diminish, AB observed.

Daytime attendance is a main target for manager Ed Hutton and promotions chief Ernst A. (Woody) Meyer. Solutions have included lower ticket prices, a "guest book" promotion, a "99 cents per hour" ticket and a Wednesday and Fri-

day "date night" with all rides included in a $2 ticket. The 99-cents and $2 gimmicks are for unlimited rides, but patrons must debark if there is a waiting line.

The guest book idea calls for motels to sell discount books to their patrons in exchange for a 25-per cent consideration. Each book has a prize coupon, and a $500 drawing is set for Labor Day evening. The sum will be split between the winning patron and the establishment selling him the book.

Containing nickel ride units, the books retail at $4.50 ($6 value) and $2.25 ($3 value). As July Fourth neared, the number of sales outlets approached 100. Some were promising their clerks the $250 if they sold the lucky book, as a sales stimulus.

Promotions—An assortment of gimmicks is Ernst Meyer's stock in trade.
(AB photos)

PROMOTION A PRIME NEED
Ocean Playland Gets Down to Business

The third season for Ocean Playland may see it finally come into its own. Opening in mid-season of 1965, the superpark in Ocean City, Md., represented a ride philosophy which has not yet been put to a true test.

Like a carnival, the park consists of a nucleus of corporate-owned rides, plus an assortment of independently owned units. All tickets are sold by the corporation, and owners are paid off at week's end when they bring in their used tickets.

"We haven't had any trouble yet," the park's Oscar Carey told AB, "but we haven't had to fight any overwhelming crowds, either. This year we'll see what happens."

The park is adopting something it ought to have done in 1965—a promotion campaign to draw people away from the beaches and from the resort's downtown boardwalk sector.

Ride Prices Lowered

There are changes from the original season: last year the entire ride price structure was lowered, the most severe drop being on the Monorail. Originally 75 cents for adults and 50 for kids, it was rescaled at 40 and 20. For 1967 there are ride changes too. The Broadway Trip is gone (to Pirates World in Florida), as is the Ferris Wheel. Instead, a larger wheel (Eli) is installed, as is a Bubble Bounce, both acquired through Diversified Amusements.

The two rides are owned by the parent Ocean Playland Inc. So is the new Go-Kart Track, replacing a

booked-in Lover's Coach ride. The karts represent more action to kids of pre-adult age, Carey said. Ride tickets are now dime units, originally 5 cents.

Also accomplished is a take-over, by the corporation, of concession games. Percentage agents are employed.

A cheerful outlook is cited, partly based on the proposed convention hall for Ocean City, for which the State of Maryland has appropriated financing and the city to set aside a land parcel. Also, the future indicates a new bridge over Assawoman Bay, bringing traffic into the city at 61st St. The park is on 65th. Plans are projected by the Maryland State Road Commission.

Close Is Good Enough

The ride operators' payments are actually a redemption, based on the contracted percentage rental. Tickets are weighed and if the total is reasonably close to the operator's count, the payoff is made. Carey said no problems have arisen in this system. He is secretary-treasurer of the corporation; George Chandler is president, and James B. Caine, vice-president. Carey said:

"We had much to learn and we're still learning, but the idea is a sound one. We have two less ride concessionaires this year. There is a lot of money invested and we're going to hustle intelligently for patronage. The capacity of this park has never been strained so we're going to spend more money to find out the answers."

I. K.

Playland struggled with attendance in its early years of operation. This was not a surprise, with the park being located "up the beach" and away from where most Ocean City vacationers stayed. This pair of Amusement Business articles from the summer of 1967 describe in detail how Playland's management was attempting to draw more people to the park.

A nearly full Playland monorail train gets ready to pull into its station in the late 1960s. The ride ran clockwise around the park, and would have been moving from left-to-right in this picture. By this point in time the Turnpike Ride had taken over the the space left by the Broadway Trip. Another notable part of the image is the lack of high-rise development in northern Ocean City.

Left: Rick Machado and his older brother Ray pose in Kiddie Land with the Hennecke Auto Carousel and the Chance Old 99 Train filling out the background.

The oversized rooster was part of Playland's menagerie of fiberglass animals. Positioned throughout the park, these critters were all made by the same company that made Playland's pirate, the International Fiberglass Co. of Venice, CA.

Right: Ray Machado and an unidentified rider take a turn on the Old 99 Train.

Left: Ray and Rick wait their turn for a spin on Playland's Antique Cars. The images on this page are all courtesy of Rick Machado. Rick ended up working at Playland from 1975-80, running just about every ride in the park.

- Ocean City Only Picnic Area
- Delmarva's Largest Amusement Park
- An Ocean Of Rides
- Fun For Everyone

PLAYLAND
AMUSEMENT PARK
65TH STREET
OCEAN CITY, MD.
FREE PARKING
FREE ADMISSION
FREE PICNIC PARK

PLAYLAND
AMUSEMENT PARK
65TH STREET
OCEAN CITY, MD.
FREE PARKING
FREE ADMISSION
FREE PICNIC PARK

FREE COUPON
$2.00 Worth $2.00
THIS COUPON WHEN PRESENTED BY AN ADULT, ENTITLES BEARER AND ENTIRE FAMILY TO ONE FREE RIDE ON THE FABULOUS
Sky Monorail
FREE COUPON

Two girls smile for the camera during a trip on the Sky Ride.

A posed photo from a Playland brochure. Bikinis were allowed on the go-karts, but bare feet were not.

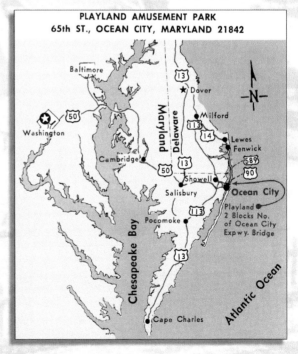

PLAYLAND AMUSEMENT PARK
65th ST., OCEAN CITY, MARYLAND 21842

Looking east from Playland's elevated monorail station toward Kiddie Land and the front of the park. The park pirate is still a pirate, and the Hennecke Auto Carousel is still part of the ride lineup (top left). That places the image in the late-1960s/early 1970s period.

PLAYLAND

AMUSEMENT PARK
A division of Larmar Corporation
65th Street, Ocean City, Maryland 21842

You'll have much more Fun

A breathtaking view of the bay from the fabulous SATELLITE MONORAIL.

42 RIDES AND ATTRACTIONS designed to please all ages and offering hours of hilarious fun and laughter for the young at heart in the clean air of beautiful Ocean City. Located only two blocks from the ocean, and the east coast's greatest beach. Playland is a must for the Ocean City visitor, guaranteeing memories of fun filled relaxation.

The great variety of Playland's rides and attractions have a rewarding appeal to the little tots, with an outstanding KIDDIELAND. For the teenagers, THE HURRICANE ROLLER COASTER, new, whirling dirvish ROTOR, lightning fast MONSTERMOUSE, a mix-up of fun on the screaming SCRAMBLER (to name only a few) and for all ages, the

challenge of CIRCUS MINIATURE GOLF, a panoramic ride on the SATELLITE MONORAIL, a soaring trip on the ALPINE SKY RIDE, or a nostalgic ride on an authentic, antique MERRY-GO-ROUND with the wooden, hand carved horses produced just after the turn of the century. There are many more thrill-packed rides, promising everyone hours of exhilarating fun. FREE PARKING for over 3000 cars. Playland Amusement Park, with Delmarva's greatest fun package. Where, FOR A MODERATE ADMISSION PRICE to the park, YOU MAY RIDE THE RIDES AS MANY TIMES AS YOU LIKE during your visit FOR NO ADDITIONAL CHARGE . . . A funtastic savings . . . Unrivaled on Delmarva.

dp MADE BY DEXTER PRESS, INC. WEST NYACK, NEW YORK   Pub. by C. H. Echols, Jr., 3307 Yorkway, Baltimore, Md. 21222

The 1970s

Ocean City boomed with development in the early 1970s, filling the vacant sandy blocks surrounding Playland with hotels, shopping centers, and restaurants. And to the north of the park, towering condo buildings were overtaking the beachfront, with the resulting row of glittering Miami Beach-inspired structures being dubbed the "Gold Coast." Helping fuel this growth was the Route 90 Bridge, which opened in 1971 and offered a new point of entry into the resort. In addition to making the northern sections of Ocean City easier to reach, the bridge merged into Coastal Highway at 62nd Street – just three convenient blocks south of Playland's entrance.

But the Route 90 Bridge did much more than lead vacationers to Playland's front door. It provided the park with an unprecedented dose of free advertising. That's because Playland was the most prominent Ocean City landmark for anyone riding

eastward across the new causeway, especially when the park was lit up at night and the twinkling outline of the Hurricane filled the eastern horizon.

Another outcome of Ocean City's development was that Playland now sat almost at the mid-point of the resort. So vacationers staying in the northern parts of town could get an amusement park fix without negotiating the ever-increasing Coastal Highway traffic to Jolly Roger on 30th Street, or all the way to Trimper's Rides at the south end of town.

Changes had taken place at the park, too. The most noticeable change, from the outside at least, was the transformation of the park's pirate into a clown. (Or maybe he was a jester – it was hard to tell.) Somehow, through a new paint job and the ambitious application of uncounted layers of fiberglass, Playland's towering mascot had been stripped of his distinctive pirate persona. Clown makeup had been painted over his bearded face,

Playland as it looked in the mid-1970s. The new Route 90 Bridge (upper left), was bringing more vacationers than ever into Ocean City, and Playland turned its iconic pirate into a ball-juggling jester. There are also new rides in the park, the most notable being the Rotor rising up just to the right of the newly-painted coaster. The Hurricane would wear its vivid shade of yellow until the park closed in 1980.

Photo by R. C. Pulling. Published by HPS Inc. Dover, Del. 19901. Printed by Dexter Press West Nyack, New York.

and a long, striped stocking cap curved sideways off of his head. Puffy polka dot-sleeves hid his once muscular arms, while red-and-white-striped balloon-at-the-bottom genie pants finished off his jarring new ensemble.

And just below his feet, another change was visible. Missing from the expansive sign over the front gate was the word "Ocean." From now on the park would simply be known as "Playland."

Changes had taken place inside the park as well. The Lover's Coach and Broadway Trip only lasted a single season, with both rides gone by the summer of 1966. And Kiddie Land suffered an exodus of rides throughout the late 1960s. The Old 99 Train, Tank Ride, Fire Trucks, Pony Carts, Hampton Motorcycles, and Hennecke Auto Carousel were all missing from Playland as the new decade began. (They weren't replaced – management chose to fill the vacant space with benches and picnic tables.) At the back of the park, actually behind the park out in the bay, the pen for the Ocean Trip Boat Ride was

empty. It's likely that maintenance costs and liability issues were behind the attraction's demise.

But there were a number of new rides in Playland. A Chance Rotor now stood like a rocket ship next to the Hurricane, flanked by a gleaming new Eli Bridge Scrambler. And spinning and rumbling just to the north of the Sky Ride loading platform were the distinctive clamshell-shaped red cars of a Tilt-A-Whirl. Speaking of new, the Hurricane Coaster had gotten a coat of bright yellow paint. Its loading platform and walkways finished off the updated look with a bold shade of orange.

Some rides swapped places. The Hot Rod cars were now running on a longer track next to the Ghost Ship, taking over the area where the Broadway Trip and Airborne once resided. The ride had a new name – the Turnpike – and the new track layout included an extended straightaway that ran behind the Ghost Ship. Filling the hole left by the Hot Rods was the displaced Airborne ride. The new Scrambler helped fill this hole, too.

One significant yet not visible change was that Playland had given up on the "booked in" ride concept. It wasn't very profitable, convincing park management that things would be easier if they took over the ownership of each and every ride, and the Old Pro Golf. (Food stands and games continued to be individually owned.)

A final change was the termination of the free admission policy. In previous years visitors could come into the park for free and buy tickets to get on the rides. Now, everyone had to pay a fee to get inside. The choices were a one price ticket that gave visitors a hand stamp and total access to the park, riding all the rides as many times as they wanted. Or a modest general admission fee that let visitors in the park without a stamp, and required that they buy tickets to get on a ride. Old Pro Golf was included in the reduced general admission fee.

Playland's ride lineup remained pretty much unchanged until 1978 when, thanks to ongoing go-kart war with Jolly Roger and Grand Kart on Route 50, the park built an L-shaped go-kart track in the front corner of the parking lot. This allowed Playland to claim that it had "the largest go-kart track in Ocean City," making the park a destination for go-kart aficionados. A single fee allowed anyone who was tall enough to ride the go-karts all day and all night. It was an Ocean City bargain that was hard to beat.

Taking over the space where the go-karts had been was a brand new Eyerly Spider. Outfitted in a menacing black and neon-green color scheme, it was the first ride guests saw once they passed the Ferris wheel. Thanks to this prime location the Spider had a significant line on most summer evenings.

One of the best places to get an overlook of the park and Ocean City was from the Hurricane loading platform. This view played a large part in making the coaster a fun place to work.

Photo by Don Ceppi. Mardelva Distributors. Inc., Salisbury, MD.

A look at the back of the park in the early 1970s, showing the position of the Rotor beside the Hurricane. Visible between the Monster Mouse and the Ghost Ship is the turnaround loop of the Turnpike.

A view of the Hurricane from the Route 90 Bridge. Karl Schwarz Playland archive.

The Hurricane

The Hurricane was Playland's centerpiece and most iconic ride. That was true from the day the park gates first opened in 1965 when the newly built wooden coaster gave Playland a defining feature unlike anything at Trimper's or Jolly Roger. And that still held true when the park closed in 1980. There was nothing else like the Hurricane in Ocean City or on the entire Eastern Shore, with the next nearest wooden coasters being hours away in Hershey Park (PA) or Wildwood, NJ.

When the Hurricane was being assembled in the spring of 1965, it held the distinction of being the first-ever wooden coaster to ever stand in Ocean City. Few at the time would have believed that 55 years later, the ride would also have the

distinction of being the *only* wooden coaster to ever stand on the resort's barrier island sands.

In coaster terms, the Hurricane was on the small side. Yet it still was the largest ride in Playland, taking up the entire southwestern corner of the park. It was also the largest ride in Ocean City, a landmark that was visible from miles away on Coastal Highway, a striking vision of white after the sun went down and the lights illuminating the ride's outline spilled into the 65th Street night sky.

According to *Amusement Business*, the Hurricane's compact figure-eight layout was 350-feet long by 40-feet high, with 1300 feet of track. The ride's wooden frame was built from plans supplied by the National Amusement Device Company, which was a prominent manufacturer of

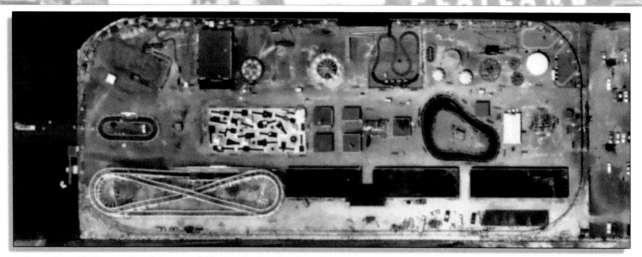

A rare late-1960s overhead image of Playland, showing just how much of the park the Hurricane occupied. The Broadway Trip and the Lover's Coach rides are already gone from the ride lineup. Karl Schwarz Playland archive.

roller coaster parts. National Amusement also provided the cars for the coaster, with Playland buying two of the company's distinctive art-deco Century Flyer trains. Each silver train had three cars apiece, with the lead car having an eye-catching tri-headlight configuration.

Walking up the long ramp to the loading platform was always an exciting thing to do, even when I was working the ride. There was such an impressive panoramic view of the park up there, a view that remained awesome even when I was counting passengers (18 was the max). And of course, there were amazing views of Ocean City once you were on the ride, with the best coming during the banked 180° horseshoe turn at the top of the lift hill. Riders could see for miles as they coasted gently into the Hurricane's first drop – across the bay to the mainland, all up and down the Ocean City coastline, and even out to the blue-green of the Atlantic Ocean.

After the coaster train accelerated down the main hill, all glimpses of your surroundings were fleeting. Yes, the Hurricane was small, but it still packed a punch, both in airtime and g-forces. One of the things I'll always remember is the framework vibrating under my feet as the cars made their way around the layout. In those moments the ride seemed alive, like it was a living entity of wood and steel.

By 1980 the Hurricane had gotten a little crotchety, with the cars often needing a push to get onto the lift chain. I never participated in the trickiest part of the ride – setting the brake to stop the coaster train after it finished its run. When the cars came rumbling out of the final turn there really wasn't a whole lot of track left to get them stopped, so it took an expert pull on the chest-high orange wooden brake lever to land the train right in front of the next set of waiting riders.

I always felt a great sense of pride during my shifts on the Hurricane. The ride was a piece of Ocean City's history, one of the town's true landmarks. Anytime that I stood on its elevated platform in my Playland uniform, I knew I'd made it to the "major leagues" of ride running.

How the Hurricane looked from the elevated monorail station on the north side of the park. This is a late 60s/early 70s image, as the coaster still has its original coat of white paint. The loading area and the track of the Turnpike Ride fills out the bottom right of the photo.

Playland's National Amusement Device tri-headlight Century Flyer coaster train.

A full coaster train takes on the main Hurricane hill in 1978. Courtesy of The Ocean City Life-Saving Station Museum, Ocean City, Maryland.

Two rare mid-1970s images of Playland's Hurricane, including a look up the lift hill.

Top Right: *Playland's Airborne ride spinning in the sunshine.* **Main Photo:** *The Airborne awaits takeoff as the ride operator checks the restraint bars. Judging by the daytime crowd, it looks like a corporate picnic was in the park. Courtesy of The Ocean City Life-Saving Station Museum, Ocean City, Maryland.*

51

Ghost Ship

Courtesy of Brandon Seidl

Playland's **Ghost Ship** has gone on to legendary status in the decades since the park's closure. That's because the ride was designed by Bill Tracy, who amusement park historians consider "the king of dark rides." During the 1960s Tracy designed more than 40 dark rides for amusement parks around the country, including Trimper's Haunted House. And as they've unceremoniously disappeared through the years, it's become clear that the Ghost Ship may have been one of the most ambitious pieces in the Tracy dark ride legacy.

The Ghost Ship was a two-story warehouse-sized building that sat next to the Monster Mouse on Playland's north midway. It caught your attention from almost anywhere in the park, as it was hard to miss the ride's haunting roofline façade, which featured a splintered and sail-less wooden galleon being devoured by a giant skeleton-faced crab. Adding menace to the bizarre creature were a pair of glowing orange eyes, and a head that tilted back and forth all night long. Sometime during its life, the skeleton face had been crowned with a head of seaweed-like hair. But this disintegrated through the years leaving just bushy plugs. By the late 1970s the skull looked like the victim of a bad hair transplant.

Inside the building, smooth moving miniature "coffin" cars guided riders through an extended black-light creep-fest of Tracy's diabolical mechanical dioramas. The most notorious and startling was a ghoulish pirate whose disembodied head slid down a wire directly at your car.

One of the unique features of the Ghost Ship

came at the halfway point of your "swim" through the haunted galleon. There your car would bust through a set of wooden doors and suddenly be outside in the night air on a section of track that ran on the roof of the loading area. This unusual perch gave you a great view of the park. And it also gave you time to catch your breath before completing the journey through Tracy's twisted vision of Davy Jones' locker.

I didn't have the opportunity to run the Ghost Ship during my summer at Playland, but I did get to ride through it a handful of times. While it was still a blast, the mechanical pieces of the ride were now 15-years-old. They hadn't aged particularly well, and were in need of almost nightly maintenance. It also didn't help that the original realistic look of Tracy's dioramas had been covered over with hastily applied layers of neon-colored spray paint. Yes, everything glowed, but the dioramas had lost their sinister edge.

Another issue the for the ride was the low-slung design of the coffin cars. Because they didn't have any type of restraint system, riders would sometimes get out of the cars and walk around inside the Ghost Ship (a "runner" was the technical park term). This was a dangerous thing to do, considering all the moving hydraulic parts and electrical circuits inside the ride. And through the years, this activity morphed from mostly good-natured curiosity into the realm of malicious – the ride was actually being vandalized. It got so bad that chain link fencing was put up along almost the entire route inside the ride. Unfortunately, at least in 1980, the Ghost Ship felt more like a bizarre black-light zoo than a haunted pirate ship.

But just as riders could get out and move around inside the ride, Playland employees could too. The mischievous young clean-up crew guys, who had access to every corner of the park, would sometimes emerge from the darkness in their glowing yellow Playland shirts to give Ghost Ship riders a scare they'd never forget.

I'm happy to report that the Ghost Ship is something from Playland that lives on, as pieces of the ride were incorporated into Trimper's Haunted House in 1989. There's also a wonderful Ghost Ship web page with dozens of photos run by good friend Brandon Seidl (www.ochh.net). Brandon lent his photos and expertise to this section. In addition, Brandon has co-authored two great Ocean City books, *Ocean City Oddities* and *Trimper's Rides.* Both are worth having in your Ocean City library.

The unique upper deck section of track above the loading area.

The images on the following pages are courtesy of John Coleman and the National Amusement Park Historical Association. They originally appeared in Volume 24, Number 6, of the NAPHA News in 2002. NAPHA's Josh Litvik and Greg Van Gompel also played a vital role in securing these priceless images.

They all appear to have been taken in the late 1970s during the offseason. It's possible they were taken after Playland's closure in 1980, but there's nothing definitive in the images to indicate that the park was being disassembled.

Why Playland's monorail is parked behind the park's jester and sign – instead of in the monorail station – is a mystery. It's also a mystery as to how the driver would have gotten off the ride and back onto the ground.

A rare image of the entire Monster Mouse. At this later point in the ride's life the "Monster Mouse" sign has been moved from its original location high over the back straightaway to the front framework of the main hill (on left). All the photos in this spread are courtesy of John Coleman and the National Amusement Park Historical Association.

Crew

A partial gathering of the Playland crew in 1979. Courtesy of Tammy Hosier Betterton.

Working at Playland was the best job I ever had. That's a simple fact. I'm not alone in this feeling, either. Other Playland alumni I talked with over the last couple of years feel the same way. We all realize that the park was a very special place, occupying a special place in time. Not only in Ocean City history, but in our own personal history as well.

A lot of things went into making Playland a great place to have a job. First, the park sat on a man-made finger of sand that pointed westward out into Assawoman Bay. That made it a universe unto itself, essentially a private Ocean City enclave. That probably wasn't an unusual quality when Playland first opened its gates in 1965. But it was a rare Ocean City feature by the time I punched in for my first shift in 1980.

Thanks to this stunning setting we had shimmering bay-reflected sunshine, sea breezes to make the day shifts feel not so hot (usually), and the best sunsets in all of Ocean City. And those sunsets were epic if you were running one of the rides in the back of the park. Watching the western sky go through an entire Crayola 64 Box of orange shadings as the lights of our spinning rides spilled into the expanding darkness...it was magic. What I wouldn't give for just one more Playland evening shift! (With my 20-year-old hair and waistline.)

The next thing that made working at Playland special was that there wasn't any extensive pre-opening preparation or lengthy post-closing clean up when a shift was finished. You got to your ride 15 minutes before opening, turned on the power, and put the ride through its paces to make sure it

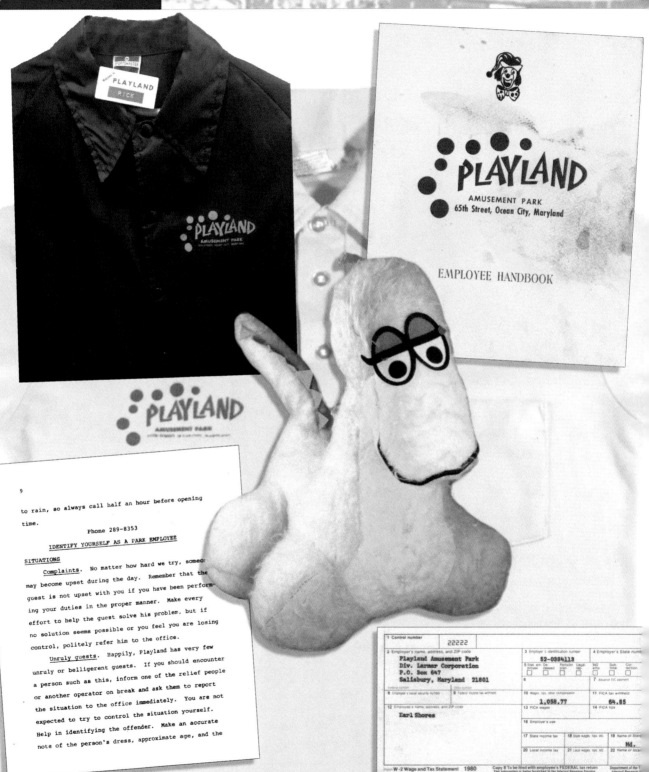

PLAYLAND

PLAYLAND
AMUSEMENT PARK
65th Street, Ocean City, Maryland

EMPLOYEE HANDBOOK

9

to rain, so always call half an hour before opening
time.

                    Phone 289-8353
        IDENTIFY YOURSELF AS A PARK EMPLOYEE

SITUATIONS

      Complaints. No matter how hard we try, someone
may become upset during the day. Remember that the
guest is not upset with you if you have been perform-
ing your duties in the proper manner. Make every
effort to help the guest solve his problem, but if
no solution seems possible or you feel you are losing
control, politely refer him to the office.

      Unruly guests. Happily, Playland has very few
unruly or belligerent guests. If you should encounter
a person such as this, inform one of the relief people
or another operator on break and ask them to report
the situation to the office immediately. You are not
expected to try to control the situation yourself.
Help in identifying the offender. Make an accurate
note of the person's dress, approximate age, and the

1 Control number	22222				
2 Employer's name, address, and ZIP code			3 Employer's identification number		4 Employer's State numb
Playland Amusement Park			52-0384113		
Div. Lerner Corporation			5 Stat. em De- Pension Legal 942 Sub- Cor-		
P.O. Box 647			ployee ceased plan rep emp total rection		
Salisbury, Maryland 21801					
Federal number	State number		6		7 Advance EIC payment
8 Employee's social security number	9 Federal income tax withheld		10 Wages, tips, other compensation		11 FICA tax withheld
			1,058.77		64.85
12 Employee's name, address, and ZIP code			13 FICA wages		14 FICA tips
Earl Shores					
			16 Employer's use		
			17 State income tax	18 State wages, tips, etc.	19 Name of State
					Md.
			20 Local income tax	21 Local wages, tips, etc.	22 Name of loca
Form W-2 Wage and Tax Statement 1980		Copy B To be filed with employee's FEDERAL tax return This information is being furnished to the Internal Revenue Service.			Department of the T Internal Revenue

A range of Playland employee goodies including a jacket, employee handbook, a W-2,
and a stuffed dinosaur prize that came from one of the park's games of chance.

was working properly. Then at the end of the night, you turned off the lights, turned off the power, secured the ride's front gate, and walked to the employee lounge to punch out. If something wasn't working properly, you told one of the relief crew or the park mechanics (Moon and Melvin) so things could be checked out before the next shift.

A third thing that made working at Playland special were the hours. On a lot of days, especially early in the summer, the park didn't open until 6:00 pm. So not only could you enjoy a full day on the beach, you also had plenty of "wiggle room" if you'd been out the night before overindulging in Ocean City's nightlife. And during those early summer shifts when park attendance was light, we often closed at 10:00 pm, giving us plenty of Ocean City night to enjoy. The only drawback to this early summer setup were the slim paychecks. But they served to keep your indulgences reasonable.

The final thing that made Playland special was that it was the nicest group of people I ever worked with. And it was a varied group of people, too. Most of the ride runners, myself included, were college and high school students. But the clean-up crew consisted of 14- and 15-year-old boys (you had to be 16-years-old to run a ride). The clean-up crew spent the nights sweeping trash and keeping the park grounds clean. They also had the unenviable task of cleaning the rides out when a guest got sick. This was something I was happy to have someone else do. The funny thing was, they really didn't seem to mind this stomach-churning assignment.

At the other end of the age spectrum, some of the most experienced Playland staff were real world adults with real life jobs – a handful were teachers – that allowed them to moonlight in the park.

One of the interesting aspects of working in the park was that unless you were consistently partnered with someone at your ride, you "knew" people, but you didn't get to know them all that well. (This was especially true if you spent a significant part of the summer working out in front of the park on Ocean City's Largest Go-Kart track.)

Still, without fail, everyone I interacted with was incredibly nice. And super cool, too. There was this laid back yet enthusiastic vibe that everybody seemed to carry. They had a palpable sense of ride-running professionalism that I wanted to be part of. Making sure the guest had fun while keeping them safe was a serious business. It was something that came into very clear focus during my very first shift.

One of my favorite things about being a Playland employee happened only three times during the summer. Yet it's still one of my most cherished memories. That would be the official Crabs and Beer after-party. This management-sponsored once-a-month event took place after closing time in the park's Top 40 Club. It was such a generous Playland tradition, and something about its simplicity and "Maryland-ness" made the gesture of appreciation feel genuine. Offering your employees a supervised and safe late-night place to socialize and unwind was a thoughtful thing to do. And we appreciated the opportunity to have a civilized and comfortable night out in our own private space – chez "Club Playland" – away from the sunburned throngs packing the clubs on Coastal Highway.

Playland's monorail passes behind the jester on a 1970s summer night.

The were a number of food offerings in Playland, including a Dairy Queen.

An overlook of Playland taken from the top of the Ferris wheel in 1979. The Spider was the park's newest ride, arriving in the summer of 1978. Courtesy of Tammy Hosier Betterton.

A close-up of the Hampton Tubs-O-Fun ride, with the Antique Cars and the Tilt-A-Whirl in the background. This fantastic image is courtesy of Eddie Zaslav - and yes, that is Eddie in the tub!

Another posed photo from a Playland brochure. Yes, bikinis were allowed on the Airborne. But bare feet were not.

After

Playland's Spider operating in Ohio's Paradise Lake Amusement Park in 1982.

Those of us who worked in Playland during that final 1980 summer had no clue that the park would never reopen. Paychecks kept coming, the rides and grounds were still being kept up to their usual immaculate standards, and we were busy. And the park had been busier than the previous summer, according to Playland veterans.

But the signs were there, just a block to our south at the teeming Ocean City Municipal Complex. Playland occupied one of the biggest pieces of land in all of Ocean City, and expanding the Municipal Complex onto the 15-acre Playland parcel would be very convenient for the city. And that's exactly what happened in 1982.

The first hint that something might be up with Playland came from my roommate, who spent the summer running the park's Dairy Queen. He also happened to be my college roommate, and during the fall semester he kept checking our mailbox for his Playland bonus check. But this promised reward for working through Labor Day never arrived. (I wasn't getting one, having bugged out of the park in late August.)

Then when he returned to Ocean City for the summer of 1981, with every expectation of again being the main man at the Dairy Queen, Playland was closed. This left him unhappily toiling in the bowels of several Ocean City restaurants before giving up on the sun and sand to enroll in our school's second summer session. I'll never forget the shock of bumping into him on campus and being told of Playland's demise.

What we didn't know was that most of Playland's rides had already been sold off. And a

Playland's Sky Ride and monorail (visible down the hill) in Paradise Lake. This photo and the Spider photo (opposite) are courtesy of Trish Caldwell-Landsittel, Creator/Administrator Monroe County Ohio Memories Facebook Group.

The unfortunate and final resting place of Playland's monorail and Sky Ride. Both were abandoned in what once was the Paradise Lake Amusement Park in eastern Ohio. Paradise Lake only lasted two seasons, opening in 1981 and closing after the summer of 1982. Interstate 70 is visible in the background. Courtesy of Jim Futrell, National Amusement Park Historical Association.

Paradise Lake's overgrown remnants in 1985. The monorail track and the Sky Ride loading platform are still intact. Courtesy of Jim Futrell, National Amusement Park Historical Association.

number were up and running at the newly opened Paradise Lake Amusement Park in eastern Ohio. Photographs confirm that Playland's monorail, Spider, and Sky Ride were all part of the Paradise Lake ride lineup. Other speculative possibilities arise from a theme park preview article that appeared in the *New York Times* on Memorial Day of 1981. According to the *Times*, Paradise Lake was going to have two Ferris wheels and two roller coasters. So perhaps Playland's Monster Mouse and Ferris wheel also ended up in Ohio.

Paradise Lake's announced ambitions were to be a sprawling multi-section destination theme park like Kings Islands or Busch Gardens. But the park opened a month behind schedule on July 1, 1981, and reportedly in an incomplete state. It had four distinct sections, or "paradises" - the Western Paradise, Children's Paradise, the Sports Paradise, and finally the Space Paradise, where Playland's

monorail, Spider, and Sky Ride all resided. Unfortunately, it was obvious to visitors right from the start that Paradise Lake had been done on the cheap. And owing to both shaky and dodgy financial underpinnings, the park only stayed open for a season and a half, closing for good at the end of the 1982 summer.

When Paradise Lake's rides were finally auctioned off in the fall of 1983, there were no takers on the monorail, or the support structure of the Sky Ride. This consigned the once featured Playland attractions to the sad fate of being abandoned to rot away in an overgrown field just off Interstate 70. I'm grateful to Jim Futrell of the National Amusement Park Historical Association for sharing the series of heartbreaking photos he took of the monorail and the forsaken remnants of Paradise Lake in 1985. All these years later they are still devastating to look at.

Another view of the final resting place of Playland's monorail. Paradise Lake's loading platform was bare bones with no shade. Courtesy of Jim Futrell, National Amusement Park Historical Association.

Back in Ocean City, the city officially purchased the Playland property in January of 1982. During the earliest days of the city's takeover a good bit of the park's infrastructure was still standing. This included the buildings that housed the games of chance, the Ghost Ship building (Trimper's had purchased the Bill Tracy interior), the Hurricane, and also the Playland sign with the jester still attached.

Once the city got serious about reconfiguring the Playland lot, the jester was sold to the Magic Forest Amusement Park in Lake George, New York. He stood there – on the ground this time – from 1987 until 2018, when new owners took over the park and sold him off. But as of 2020 he still has life, and is being prepped for a resurrection by Atlantis Plumbing in Dallas, Georgia.

The coaster, unfortunately, did not go on to a second life. It was disassembled and the lumber auctioned off, with some of it going to frame a house in the Ocean City area.

Forty years on there's not much left to remind us of Playland's existence. Ghost Ship pieces can still be seen in Trimper's Haunted House, and the Amusement Park History Museum has a beautifully restored Ghost Ship car as part of its collection. The concrete mooring that held the Sky Ride turnaround tower is still a marine hazard in the bay at 65th Street, and hopefully by the time this book is published the Playland Muffler Man jester will be standing tall in Georgia.

Otherwise, all we have are the memories, which grow dimmer with each passing year. But hopefully this book will keep them refreshed, and help us all relive those warm summer nights when the glow of Playland filled the Ocean City night sky...and anything seemed possible.

Ghost Ship

Hurricane Coaster

Playland Jester

Playland Sign

Go-kart Track

O.C. buys amusement park

OCEAN CITY, Md. (AP) — Ocean City officials have decided to put a former amusement facility to work for the city government.

Located on about 15 acres of land along the Chesapeake Bay, the former "Playland" is due for approximately $1.4 million in new construction --a computerized fueling station, a bus-storage facility and a vehicle-maintenance building.

City officials said the primary purpose in obtaining the property, which was purchased for $1.49 million in January 1982, was to centralize a public works system now spread around the resort city.

The fueling station will cost an estimated $150,000 to build, while the vehicle-maintenance building will cost $600,000.

The city is due to open bidding this week for construction of the vehicle maintenance facility, a 10,000-square-foot building that will also provide warehouse and office space.

The last building to be constructed is a storage facility for the town's bus fleet. A $650,000 Mass Transit Administration bond will pay for that facility.

An airplane view of Playland in 1983 after Ocean City took over the property and expanded the Municipal Complex. The outline of the go-kart track is still visible, and the Ghost Ship building and the Hurricane are still standing. Also still standing were the park offices and the buildings that housed Playland's games of chance. In the center of the photo you can still see the Playland sign and the ghostly yellow outline of Playland's jester. In 1987 he was sold to the Magic Forest in Lake George, New York.

Playland's jester/clown as he appeared in the Magic Forest Amusement Park (Lake George, New York). He was part of the park from 1987-2018, and now resides at the Atlantis Plumbing Company in Dallas, Georgia.

One of the last remaining ride pieces of Playland is this beautifully restored Ghost Ship car. It's part of the American Amusement Park Museum's extensive collection of "lost" rides. Courtesy of the American Amusement Park Museum.

The "original" Ocean City Playland, late 1960s.

Ocean City Pier, August 1967.

Trimper's, August 1974.

Jolly Roger, early 1970s.

Final Thoughts

This book is really the finish of the dream that started with *Playland: Greetings From Ocean City, Maryland*. In that book, I reconstructed the park with words, something that turned out to be the biggest writing challenge I've ever faced.

For *Playland In Photos*, the park images are plain for everyone to see. Even the photos that are not in perfect focus bring something special to the book. Sort of like our actual distant memories of Playland, which get fuzzier with each passing year, yet we cherish the fact that they still exist.

It was gratifying to have the opportunity to assemble all of these Playland images in one place. And it's something I couldn't have done without the help of some very special people.

This book wouldn't have happened without the encouragement and support of friend and fellow Playland co-worker Rich Machado. I'm also grateful to Brandon Seidl for generously sharing his Playland and Ocean City resources, and wish him great success with *Ocean City Oddities*. Josh Litvik and Jim Futrell from the National Amusement Park Historical Association made invaluable contributions to the book, providing both support and rare Playland materials. A big "thank you" to the American Amusement Park Museum for their help and Playland preservation work. And one of the pleasant surprises was making the acquaintance of Karl Schwarz, who freely shared his personal Playland archive.

As always, I'm grateful for Robin and Andy, who propped me up and pushed me forward when the "doubts" crept in.

I hope that *Playland In Photos* allowed you to touch a distant and cherished time. And if you're looking for additional Ocean City reading material, check out the titles listed on the right. See you in OC!

Earl Shores

My personal on-the-ground story of what is was like to work in Playland during its final summer.

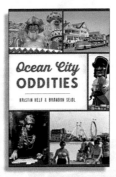

Brandon Seidl and Kristin Helf take a historical look at Ocean City's one-of-a-kind attractions.

Ocean City historian Bunk Mann's second stunning coffee table hardback of rare historical images.

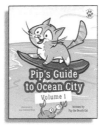

Pip, the coolest cat to ever step on the sand, gives young and young at heart readers a tour of all the things that make Ocean City great!

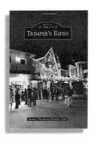

Monica Thrash and Brandon Seidl chronicle the amazing history of Trimper's Rides